PALESTINIAN OBJECTS AT THE UNIVERSITY OF MINNESOTA

by

William D. E. Coulson

Introduction

A collection of 66 vases, 8 lamps, 5 figurines, and a group of miscellaneous sherds, of which the two best (P-12, P-13) are included in this catalogue, forms part of a recent bequest to the University of Minnesota by the late Andrew J. Sarazyn of Marshall, Minnesota. Mr. Sarazyn served for many years with the United Nations in the Middle East. The process of restoring and identifying the vases and figurines was undertaken during a seminar sponsored by the Department of Classics and conducted in the Fall of 1980.[1] The University had already in its possession, as a result of its partial sponsorship of the excavations at Tel Mikhal, ten vases from the excavations of Tel Aviv University at Beer-Sheba.[2] Since the objects from the Sarazyn bequest have been identified by means of parallels as originating in Palestine, the ten vases from Beer-Sheba are, for the sake of completeness, included in this catalogue. It was decided to publish only those vases of Palestinian origin in this catalogue, since they form a clearly homogeneous body of material.

1. Five students in the Classics Department's archaeology program participated in the seminar. These students are, in alphabetical order: Elizabeth Fisher, Jessica Greenberg, Dianne Johnson, Edward Lee, and Eugene Pertler. The author also wishes to thank Vice-President Keller of the University of Minnesota for permission to publish these objects from the Sarazyn bequest.

2. These ten vases are housed on the Minneapolis campus in the University Art Museum. Ten additional vases were sent to the University of Minnesota at Duluth; because of their similarity in form to the Minneapolis vases, those at Duluth have not been included in this catalogue. The author is indebted to Professor Ze'ev Herzog, Institute of Archaeology, Tel Aviv University, for his kindness in arranging to have the Beer-Sheba vases sent to the University of Minnesota and also wishes to thank him and Lili Singer for their careful reading of this manuscript and for their helpful suggestions for its improvement. The author also wishes to thank Professor Kathleen Warner Slane of the Department of Art History and Archaeology at the University of Missouri at Columbia who has offered valuable suggestions on the Hellenistic and Roman sections of this catalogue.

The importance of the Sarazyn Collection is that it spans a broad period of time from the Early Bronze Age to the Byzantine era and presents an excellent survey of the various vessel types from each period and adds to the published corpus of Palestinian objects, primarily pottery, to be found in North American collections. Specifically, it adds to the catalogue of Palestinian wares published by Hayes in his Roman Pottery in the Royal Ontario Museum (Toronto 1976).

The collection is also quite interesting, for it contains a number of unusual vases, for which no known direct parallels exist. With the exception of the middle bronze incense burner (P-8) which may be a clay copy of an alabaster prototype, all the unusual shapes belong to either the Hellenistic or Roman periods and probably represent Palestinian imitations and derivations from standard forms. The carinated cup (P-40) may have been derived from either Attic spheroid cups or from Hellenistic household vessels which have the same incurved sides and carinated bodies. The amphoriskos (P-44) has a fusiform-shaped body and combines the unguentarium shape with the neck handles of a small amphora. The shape of P-53 may represent a Palestinian imitation of the piriform unguentarium type; lilkewise, P-54 may be a more angular variation of the piriform type. The ribbed unguentaria (P-55, P-56) are quite unusual and do not exist elsewhere in clay. Their rippled contours, however, suggest that they may have been copied from blown glass shapes, most especially the balsamarium. The bulbous and angular shape of P-57 has probably been derived from the bulbous unguentarium type but with a more flaring body and wider neck. The shape of the ribbed juglet (P-68) is also quite unusual and without ceramic parallels; it, too, may have been derived from glass prototypes or may have been copied from the small ribbed ceramic jars popular in late Roman times. To the lamp category belongs a medium-sized vessel (L-8) of untypical design, dated here as Byzantine because of a fragment of green glaze preserved on the body near the handle. The female figurines (F-2, F-3) forming parts of incense burners, whereas not uncommon, yet may be noted as distinctive.

The catalogue has been divided into three major sections: I. Vases; II. Lamps; and, III. Figurines. In each section, the objects are listed under their main chronological divisions, and at the end of each entry parallels have been cited. In some cases exact parallels do not exist; wherever this occurs, the nearest possible parallel is cited, and the words "related to" are used. To denote derivations from standard forms, the words "derived from" have been used. All objects have been arranged chronologically. Within these broad chronological divisions (Bronze Age, Iron Age, Hellenistic, Roman, and Byzantine), the vases have been arranged according to shape, beginning in each section with the open shapes and ending with the closed ones. The intent of such an arrangement is to enable the reader to perceive the variety and range of shapes within each chronological period. Also for convenience and ease of identification, all vessel profiles and drawings of objects have been arranged so that the Bronze and Iron Age pots appear in Figs. 1 and 2, the Hellenistic and Roman vases in Fig. 3, the lamps in Fig. 4, and the figurines in Fig. 5. In all cases where it occurs, slip or wash has been indicated in the profiles by the device of hatching and bands of paint by solid black lines.

CATALOGUE

I. VASES

Bronze Age

P-1 Bowl. Fig. 1

Intact. H.0.078, D. rim 0.222, D. base 0.143. Handmade, but finished on wheel. Clay and slip Munsell 5YR 7/8 reddish yellow. Semi-coarse fabric with small white grit. Uneven pock-marked surface. Remnants of reddish yellow slip on interior. Combed decoration on outer rim.
EB IV - MB I.
cf. O. Tufnell, Lachish IV, The Bronze Age (Oxford 1958) pl. 66.431.

P-2 Bowl. Fig. 1

Intact. H. 0.068, D. rim 0.16. Wheelmade. Clay Munsell 5YR 6/6 reddish yellow; slip 10YR 8/4 very pale brown. Semi-coarse farbic with white and black grit. Wheel marks on surface; rounded base. Traces of slip on interior.
MB I.
cf. R. Amiran, Ancient Pottery of the Holy Land (Jerusalem 1969) 86-7, pl. 23.8 (from el-Ḥusn).

P-3 Bowl. Fig. 1

Intact. H. 0.062, D. rim 0.235, D. base 0.08. Clay 5YR 7/6 reddish yellow. Semi-coarse fabric with white and red grit. Surface rough, with pock and wheel marks.
MB IIA.
cf. G. Loud, Megiddo II (Chicago 1948) pl. 14.17 (Mediggo XIV).

P-4 Bowl. Fig. 1

Missing section of rim and upper body; restored. H. 0.102, W. 0.127, D. rim 0.109, D. base 0.042. Clay 7.5YR 6/6 reddish yellow. Semi-coarse fabric with white grit. Surface rough, with pock and wheel marks.
MB-IIA.
cf. G. Loud, Megiddo II, pl. 14.28 (Megiddo XIV).

P-5 Small goblet. Fig. 1

Intact. H. 0.075, D. rim 0.06, D. base 0.03. Clay and slip 7.5YR 7/8 reddish yellow. Fine clay with micaceous inclusions. Shallow body with slightly rounded walls; ringed base, everted rim. Slipped.
MB IIB-C.
Related to Loud, _Megiddo_ II, pl. 28.11 (Megiddo XII).

P-6 Goblet. Fig. 1

Intact. H. 0.124, D. rim 0.063, D. base 0.070. Clay 7.5YR 7/6 reddish yellow. Semi-coarse flaky clay with fine grit and possible fibrous inclusions. Light brown core. Semi-smooth to rough encrusted surfaces. Interior finger grooves; flat base.
MB I.
cf. O. Tufnell, _Lachish_ IV, pl. 67.464.

P-7 Goblet. Fig. 1

Intact. H. 0.105, D. rim 0.061, D. base 0.0508. Clay 5YR 6/5 reddish yellow. Semi-coarse flaky clay with fine grit and possible fibrous inclusions. Pinkish brown core. Vessel fired red on one side. Rough encrusted surface fractured with exterior and interior fissures. Flat base.
MB I.
cf. Amiran, 85, pl.22.15 (Kh. Samiya); O. Tufnell, _Lachish_ IV, pl. 67.478.

P-8 Incense burner. Fig. 1

Missing small section from body; partially restored. H. 0.035, W. 0.086, D. rim 0.07, D. base 0.048. Clay 5YR 8/3 pale yellow. Rim chipped, surface eroded, with greenish oxidation. Semi-coarse, sandy fabric similar to P-9. Burnt on interior. Black paint on body below rim; black dots on rim 0.01 m. apart; some paint on handles. One hole in each handle, perhaps for tieing a flat cover. The shape is unusual and perhaps may have been copied in clay from alabaster models.
MB I?
Perhaps derived from K.M. Kenyon, _Excavations at Jericho_ II (London 1965) 221, fig. 100.14.

P-9 Teapot. Fig. 1

Intact. H. 0.086, W. 0.102, D. rim 0.08. Clay 2.5 YR 7/4 pale yellow. Semi-coarse, sandy fabric. Smooth surfaces with wheel

marks visible; rounded base.
MB I.
cf. P.L.O. Guy, Mediggo Tombs (Chicago 1938) pls. 10.4, 11.30, 12.7.

P-10 Juglet. Fig. 1

Intact. H. 0.071, D. rim 0.031, D. base 0.029. Clay Munsell 5YR 8/4 pink; paint 10YR 6/8 brownish yellow. Handmade. Semi-coarse fabric with sand and straw inclusions. Decorated on body and handle with irregular vertical stripes of paint applied by hand.
EB IIB.
cf. J.A. Callaway, The Early Bronze Age Sanctuary at ᶜAi I (London 1972) 235, fig. 55.16 (decoration); O. Tufnell, Lachish IV, pl. 58.94 (shape); related to Callaway, Early Bronze Age Sanctuary at ᶜAi, 238, fig. 56.22 (shape).

P-11 Piriform juglet. Fig. 1

Intact. H. 0.090, W. 0.059, D. rim 0.026, D. base 0.019. Clay 10YR 7/2 light grey; slip 10YR 6/2 light brownish grey. Semi-fine clay with sand-sized inclusions; some light brown incrustation; decorated with a lightly burnished slip.
MB IIB.
cf. Loud, Megiddo II, pl. 24.31 (shape), pl. 24.19 (slip) (Mediggo XII).

P-12 Body frag. of juglet. Fig. 1

H. (pres.) 0.04, W. 0.03, Est. D. 0.255. Clay and slip 10YR 5/3 brown. Semi-coarse porous fabric with fine mineral grit. Traces of slip preserved. Surface decorated with punctured design in geometric pattern typical of Tell el-Yahudiyeh ware.
MB IIA-B.
cf. Amiran, 117, pl. 36.

P-13 Body frag. of jug. Fig. 1

H. (pres.) 0.067, W. 0.06, Est. D. 0.117. Clay and slip 5YR 7/3-7/4 pink; paint 7.5R 3/4 dusky red. Fine well-fired clay with straw inclusions and mineral grit. Small pock marks on surface. Slight traces of burnish. Surface decorated with painted cross-hatched triangles and diamonds typical of Bichrome Ware.
MB IIC.
cf. Loud, Megiddo II, pl. 39.7-8 (Megiddo X).

P-14 Bilbil. Fig. 1

Intact. H. 0.141, D. 0.071, D. rim 0.035, D. base 0.036. Clay 5YR 7/6 reddish yellow; slip 7.5YR N4/0 dark grey. Semi-fine clay with micaceous inclusions; scarred surface; fired to a lighter shade on one side (7.5YR 5/2). Base-ring I ware, typical of LB I and IIA Cypriote juglets; probably Cypriote import.
LB I or IIA.
cf. Eretz-Israel, Archaeological, Historical and Geographical Studies (Israel Exploration Society VI) 35, fig. 1.8 and pl. 3 (Jerusalem).

P-15 Pilgrim flask. Fig. 1

Intact. H. 0.135, D. rim 0.029. Clay and slip 7.5YR 7/6 reddish yellow. Semi-coarse fabric with sand-sized inclusions. Belly decorated with dark brown and black concentric circles.
LB IIB.
cf. Loud, Megiddo II, pl. 67.1 (Megiddo VIIB).

P-16 Pyxis. Fig. 1

Intact. H. 0.077, D. rim 0.048, D. base 0.114. Clay 10YR 7/5 red. Wheelmade. Semi-coarse to fine clay with traces of fibrous inclusions. Reddish pink core. Wet-smoothed surface with rim and neck patchwork of brown clay. Two vertical handles joined to shoulder top contain holes for hanging. Neck, shoulder, and handles originally painted black. Decoration includes three band-combed rings at mid-belly; large dark brown band flanked by two small black stripes. Local imitation of a Mycenaean (LH IIIB) type.
LB IIB.
cf. Tufnell, Lachish IV, pl. 82.923; F.H. Stubbings, Mycenaean Pottery from the Levant (Cambridge 1951) pl. 13.4 (Enkomi),5 (Klavdia).

Iron Age

P-17 Bowl. Fig. 1

Restored. H. 0.083, D. rim 0.227, D. base 0.071. Clay 2.5YR 6/6 light red; core 5YR 6/2 pinkish grey. Semi-coarse fabric with white grit. Smooth surface with wheel marks; some pock marks. Chips on rim. Wheel burnished.
Beer-Sheba, Locus 300, registration no. 2421/1.
Iron IIC.

cf. Albright, "Beit Misrim III," AASOR 21-2 (1941-3) pl. 22.7; related to J.W. Crowfoot et al., Samaria-Sebaste III, The Objects (London 1957) 194, fig. 32.7.

P-18 Bowl. Fig. 1

Intact. H. 0.063, D. rim 0.215, D. base 0.065. Clay 7.5YR 6/6 reddish yellow; slip 10YR 4/8 red. Semi-coarse fabric with red and white grit. Smooth surface with a few pock marks; some incrustation. Slip brushed around interior, along rim, and some splashed on side.
Iron IIC.
cf. W.F. Albright, "The Excavation of Tell Beit Mirism I," AASOR 12 (1930-31) pl. 65.26.

P-19 Bowl. Fig. 1

Intact. H. 0.053, D. rim 0.136, D. base 0.032. Clay and slip 10YR 7/4 very pale brown; core 5YR 6/6 reddish yellow. Semi-coarse, powdery fabric. Rim slightly eroded; some pock marks and incrustation on body. Faint wheel marks visible. Dark and light splotches of slip on surface.
Iron IIC.
cf. E. Grant and G.E. Wright, Ain Shems Excavations IV (Haverford 1938) pl. 63.25 (Beth-shemesh IIb); related to Albright, "Beit Mirism I," AASOR 12 (1930-31) pl. 51.7; pl. 67.8.

P-20 Bowl. Fig. 1

Restored. H. 0.043, D. rim 0.151, D. base 0.075. Clay 7.5YR 6/4 light brown; core 2.5YR 6/4 light reddish brown; slip 2.5YR 4/4 reddish brown. Semi-coarse fabric with white grit. Wheel ridging visible. Slip on exterior, some on interior.
Beer-Sheba, Locus 48, registration no. 1587/1. From the western quarter, Stratum II.
Iron IIC.
Published in Y. Aharoni, Beer-Sheba I (Tel Aviv 1973) pl. 72.3.

P-21 Carinated bowl. Fig. 1

Intact. H. 0.047, D. rim 0.12, D. base 0.032. Clay 5YR 6/6 reddish yellow; slip 10YR 4/8 red. Semi-coarse fabric with white and dark grit. Smooth surface, some light incrustation; chip on rim. Slip brushed around interior, band on exterior.
Iron IIC.
cf. Albright, "Beit Mirsim I," AASOR 12 (1931-32) pl. 64.5; Lamon and Shipton, Megiddo I, pl. 28.96 (Mediggo V-III).

P-22 Miniature saucer. Fig. 1

1/3 of body missing. H. 0.016, D. rim 0.68, D. base 0.46. Clay 2.5YR 5/6 red; core 2.5YR 6/4 light reddish brown. Semi-coarse fabric with white and dark grit. Surface wet-smoothed. Wheel marks visible; string marks at base.
Iron IIC.
cf. Albright, "Beit Mirsim I," AASOR 12 (1930-31) pl. 65.19; Crowfoot et al., Samaria-Sebaste III, 140, fig. 13.4.

P-23 Chalice base. Fig. 1

H. 0.052, D. base 0.110. Clay 10YR 8/1 white. Fine, sandy fabric. Surfaces worn and eroded; evidence of wet-smoothing.
Iron IIA-B.
cf. Grant and Wright, Ain Shems IV, pl. 62.54 (Beth-shemesh IIa).

P-24 Holemouth jar. Fig. 2

Restored. H. 0.27, D. rim 0.116. Clay 7.5YR 6/4 light brown; core 2.5YR 6/4 light reddish brown. Semi-coarse fabric with white grit. Wet-smoothed surface; wheel marks visible.
Beer-Sheba, Locus 22, registration no. 138/1. From the western quarter, Stratum II.
Iron IIC.
Published in Aharoni, Beer-Sheba I, pl. 71.20.

P-25 Cooking pot. Fig. 2

Restored. H. 0.166, D. rim 0.157, W. handles 0.024. Clay 5YR 6/4 light reddish brown. Chips on rim and handles. Semi-coarse fabric with white grit. Surface wet-smoothed; burnt in areas around base. Raised bands on neck; 2 horizontal incisions at base of handles.
Beer-Sheba, Locus 77, registration no. 1615/2. From the western quarter, Stratum II.
Iron IIC.
Published in Aharoni, Beer-Sheba I, pl. 66.4.

P-26 Large cooking pot. Fig. 2

Restored. H. 0.203, D. rim 0.09, D. base 0.17. Clay 10YR 4/6 red. Semi-coarse fabric with sand-sized and small pebble inclusions. Incised lines on body and rim. Carinated body. Wheel marks visible; burnt in places on lower belly. Potter's mark in shape of "X" on handle.

Beer-Sheba, Locus 28, registration no. 1092/1. From the western quarter, Stratum II.
Iron IIC.
Published in Aharoni, Beer-Sheba I, pl. 66.13.

P-27 Decanter. Fig. 2

Restored. H. 0.194, D. 0.148, D. rim 0.052, D. base 0.062. Clay varies from 5YR 6/4 light reddish brown to 5YR 7/2 pinkish grey. Semi-coarse fabric with sand-sized and small pebble inclusions. Decorated on belly with horizontal bands made with dull instrument.
Beer-Sheba, Locus 70, registration no. 1512/3. From Stratum II.
Iron IIC.
cf. Y. Yadin, Y. Aharoni, et al., Hazor II (Jerusalem 1959) pl. 87.4 (Hazor VA).

P-28 Decanter. Fig. 2

Restored. H. 0.190, D. 0.146, D. base 0.068. Clay 2.5YR 6/8 light red. Semi-coarse fabric with sand-sized and micaceous inclusions. White incrustation on portions of vessel.
7th Cent. B.C.E.
cf. O.C. Tufnell and I.L. Harding, Lachish III, The Iron Age (Oxford 1953) pl. 87.274 (Lachish II).

P-29 Decanter. Fig. 2

Intact. H. 0.168, D. 0.074, D. rim 0.031, D. base 0.044. Clay 5YR 7/6 reddish yellow; slip 2.5YR 6/6 light red. Semi-coarse fabric with micaceous and pebble inclusions; heavy brownish-white incrustation on portions of vessel.
7th Cent. B.C.E.
cf. Tufnell and Harding, Lachish III, pl. 87.277 (Lachish II).

P-30 Juglet. Fig. 2

Intact. H. 0.141. D. rim 0.04, D. base 0.06. Clay and slip 2.5YR 6/8 light red. Semi-coarse clay with sand-sized inclusions. Elliptical shape. Surface slipped and hand burnished.
Iron IIC.
cf. Crowfoot et al., Samaria-Sebaste III, 170, fig. 23.10-11.

P-31 Dipper juglet. Fig. 2

Intact. H. 0.027, D. rim 0.022, D. base 0.015. Clay 10YR 7/3 very pale brown. Fine clay, wet-smoothed; light grey-brown

core. Piriform shape but more globular than P-32.
Beer-Sheeba, Locus 28, registration no. 1048/1. From the western quarter, Stratum II.
Iron IIC.
Published in Aharoni, Beer-Sheba, I, pl. 74.15.

P-32 Piriform juglet. Fig. 2

Intact. H. 0.121, D. rim 0.031, D. base 0.015. Clay 2.5YR 7/2 light grey. Fine clay, wet-smoothed; pale grey core. Piriform shape; tapered neck with everted pouring lip; rounded base. Traces of wheelmade finger-combing on belly.
Beer-Sheba, Locus 808, registration no. 7612/1. From Stratum II.
Iron IIC.
cf. Loud, Megiddo II, pl. 88.12 (Megiddo VA); Yadin et al., Hazor II, pl. 70.2 (Hazor VI).

P-33 Juglet. Fig. 2

Intact. H. 0.101, D. 0.071, D. rim 0.032. Clay 10YR 4/1 dark grey; slip 10YR 2/1 black. Semi-coarse fabric with micaceous inclusions; some incrustation. Black slip, faded and worn at base.
Iron IIA.
cf. Y. Aharoni, Lachish V (Tel Aviv 1975) pl. 55, Jd 10 (Lachish V).

P-34 Black dipper juglet. Fig. 2

Intact. H. 0.061, D. rim 0.016, D. base 0.008. Clay and slip 7.5YR 3/0 very dark grey. Fine clay; burnished black slip over entire vessel. Small carinated bulbous body tapered to small semi-flat base; slight everted lip with short neck.
Beer-Sheba, Locus 66, registration no. 1505/1. From the western quarter, Stratum II.
Iron IIC.
Published in Aharoni, Beer-Sheba I, pl. 69-17.

P-35 Black juglet. Fig. 2

Missing handle and neck. H. 0.045, D. rim 0.02, D. base 0.004. Clay and slip 10YR 6/8 light red. Coarse fabric with sand-sized and pebble inclusions. Small globular body; red slip.
Iron IIC.
cf. Amiran, 263, photo 264 (Beth-shemesh).

P-36 Small bottle. Fig. 2

Intact. H. 0.134, D. rim 0.063. Clay and slip 7.5YR 4/0 grey-black. Fine clay with micaceous inclusions. Small chip on rim; pointed base. Surface covered with horizontal bands of white paint. Probable Assyrian import.
7th Cent. B.C.E.
cf. G.A. Reisner, C.S. Fisher, D.G. Lyon, Harvard Excavations at Samaria 1908-1910 I (Cambridge 1924) 288, fig. 163.

P-37 Small jar. Fig. 2

Intact. H. 0.075, S. rim 0.044. Clay and slip 2.5YR 3/0 very dark grey. Semi-coarse fabric with sand-sized inclusions. Surface painted with white bands; black slipped, wheel burnished. Round base and body; off-set rim, no handles.
7th Cent. B.C.E.
Similar to P-36 in decoration, but more globular in shape.

Hellenistic

P-38 Bowl with vertical sides. Fig. 3

Restored; missing small section of rim. H. 0.049, D. rim 0.123, D. base 0.03. Clay 5YR 6/6 reddish yellow. Semi-coarse fabric, wet-smoothed. String marks at base; wheel ridging.
Late 1st Cent. B.C.E. - early 1st Cent. C.E.
cf. R. de Vaux, "Fouilles au Khirbet Qumrân: Rapport préliminaire," RB 60 (1953) 83ff., fig. 4.1-2; related to J.W. Crowfoot et al., Samaria-Sebaste III, fig. 56.9; D.W. Whitcomb and J.H. Johnson, Quesir al-Qadim 1978 (Cairo 1979) 99, pl. 33b.

P-39 Bowl with incurved rim. Fig. 3

Intact. H. 0.031, D. rim 0.063, D. base 0.003. Clay 2.5YR 7/4 pale yellow. Semi-coarse fabric with grey and white grit. Surface wet-smoothed with a few pock marks; string marks at base.
Late 1st Cent. B.C.E. - early 1st Cent. C.E.
cf. J.B. Pritchard, "The Excavation at Herodian Jericho, 1951," AASOR 32-33 (1952-54) pl. 59-37; J.W. Crowfoot et al., Samaria-Sebaste III, 265, fig. 56.10; related to W.M.F. Petrie et al., Lahun II (London 1923) pl. 61.18.

P-40 Carinated cup. Fig. 3

Intact. H. 0.054, D. rim 0.060, D. base 0.026. Clay 7/5YR 7/4 pink; slip 5YR 6/6 reddish yellow. Fine fabric, worn surfaces. Broad spheroid body; upturned rim; flat base. Reddish yellow slip. This shape is unusual and is perhaps a Palestinian variation of Attic spheroid cups.
2nd-1st Cent. B.C.E.
Perhaps derived from H.A. Thompson, "Two Centuries of Hellenistic Pottery," Hesperia 3 (1934) 373, fig. 58, D19.

P-41 Fusiform unguentarium. Fig. 3

Intact. H. 0.175, D. rim 0.025, D. base 0.026. Clay and slip 10YR 6/2 light brownish grey. Fine clay; well-smoothed body with off-set rim. Brownish grey slip; grey-black bands on shoulder and belly.
Mid-2nd Cent. B.C.E.
cf. O.V. Sellers, The Citadel of Beth-zur (Philadelphia 1933) pl. 10.14.

P-42 Fusiform unguentarium. Fig. 3

Intact. H. 0.175, D. rim 0.026, D. base 0.027. Clay and slip 10YR 7/2 light grey. Fine clay; wet-smoothed with sand-sized and micaceous inclusions. Off-set rim. Light grey creamy slip, eroded in places. Brush-combed grey bands on neck and belly.
Late 1st Cent. B.C.E.
cf. C.N. Johns, "The Citadel, Jerusalem," QDAP 14 (1950) 121ff., fig. 14.7; related to J.W. Hayes, Roman Pottery in the Royal Ontario Museum (Toronto 1976) 90, pl. 5.46.

P-43 Fusiform unguentarium. Fig. 3

Restored. H. 0.242, D. rim 0.023, D. base 0.034. Clay 2.5YR 5/8 red. Missing frags. of neck and rim; chipped at base. Fine clay, well-smoothed. Orange-red core. No slip or decoration.
Late 1st Cent. B.C.E.
cf. F.F. Jones, "Hellenistic and Roman Pottery," in H. Goldman, Excavations at Gözlü Kule, Tarsus I (Princeton 1950) fig. 135.236; related to H.S. Robinson, The Athenian Agora V, Pottery of the Roman Period (Princeton 1959) pl. 2, F 48.

P-44 Amphoriskos. Fig. 3

Intact. H. 0.172, D. rim 0.026, D. base 0.038. Clay 7.5YR 7/6

reddish yellow. Semi-coarse clay with sand-sized and small shell inclusions. Beveled and flanged rim; flat sectioned neck handles; fusiform-shaped body. P-44 is a larger example of the fusiform type represented by P-43 and P-45. Perhaps double capacity? Possibly a Palestinian variation combining the unguentarium and amphoriskos types.
2nd-1st Cent. B.C.E.
Rim related to P-43, handles to P-45.

P-45 Amphoriskos. Fig. 3

Intact. H. 0.182, D. rim 0.027, D. base 0.017. Clay 5YR 7/8 reddish yellow. Semi-coarse clay with sand-sized inclusions. Orange-red core. Fusiform body with flat base; neck handles. Plain.
Late 2nd Cent. B.C.E.
Related to Robinson, Athenian Agora V, pl. 2, F 69; Reisner et al., Samaria, 302, fig. 182a.

P-46 Jar. Fig. 3

Intact. H. 0.078, D. 0.064, D. rim 0.038, D. base 0.039. Clay 10YR 7/4-7/3 very pale brown. Semi-coarse fabric with sand-sized inclusions. Tubular neck; bulbous carinated body.
2nd Cent. B.C.E.
Related to Jones, in Goldman, Tarsus I, 227, figs. 133, 185, no. 207.

P-47 Bottle. Fig. 3

Intact. H. 0.139, D. rim 0.023, D. base 0.036. Clay and slip 7.5YR 7/2 pinkish grey. Fine clay with sand-sized inclusions. Sagging pear-shaped vessel with short, narrow neck and flat base. Light grey slip eroded in places; black and orange-brown bands on neck and shoulder.
1st Cent. B.C.E. - early 1st Cent. C.E.
cf. P.W. Lapp, Palestinian Ceramic Chronology, 200 B.C.-A.D. 70 (New Haven 1961) 166, Type 38, no. B-S.

P-48 Neck frag. of flask. Fig. 3

H. (pres.) 0.019, D. rim 0.031. Clay 5YR 8/2 white. Fine yellowish white clay; worn surfaces. Off-set rim. Plain.
1st Cent. B.C.E. - early 1st Cent. C.E.
cf. Lapp, Palestinian Ceramic Chronology, 161, Type 29.

P-49 Stamped handle. Fig. 3

L. (pres.) 0.054, D. stamp 0.007. Clay 2.5YR 8/2 white. Semi-coarse fabric with some sand-sized inclusions. Stamp of small circular rosette on knob at top of handle.
2nd-1st Cent. B.C.E.
cf. Crowfoot _et al._, _Samaria-Sebaste_ III, 259, fig. 53.6; Jones, in Goldman, _Tarsus_ I, fig. 175.497

Roman

P-50 Bowl. Fig. 3

Intact. H. 0.032, D. rim 0.119, D. base 0.04. Clay 2.5YR 3/6 dark red. Semi-coarse fabric with micaceous inclusions; heavy incrustation; chips on rim.
1st Cent. C.E.
Related to Whitcomb and Johnson, _Quesir al-Qadim 1978_, 77, pl. 22i.

P-51 Small bowl. Fig. 3

Intact. H. 0.043, D. rim 0.066, D. base 0.035. Clay and slip 5YR 4/2 dark reddish grey. Coarse fabric with sand-sized and small pebble inclusions. A few wheel marks visible on surface; very worn. Everted sides.
Late 1st Cent. B.C.E. - 1st Cent. C.E.
Related to R. de Vaux, "Fouilles de Khirbet Qumrân: Rapport preliminaire sur les 3e, 4e, et 5e campagnes," _RB_ 63 (1956) 533ff., fig. 1.13.

P-52 Small bowl. Fig. 3

Intact. H. 0.043, D. rim 0.067, D. base 0.025. Clay and slip 7.5YR 6/6 reddish yellow. Semi coarse fabric with sand-sized and small pebble inclusions. Slight wheel ridging on exterior. Everted sides.
For date and related shapes, see under P-51.

P-53 Piriform unguentarium. Fig. 3

Intact. H. 0.115, D. rim 0.023, D. base 0.021. Clay and slip 10YR 7/4 very pale brown. Slip perhaps originally red, but now quite worn. Fine clay with sand-sized and micaceous inclusions. Light buff core. Tubular neck with sharply off-set

rim; slender, ovoid body with flat base. Palestinian imitation of the piriform type.
1st Cent. C.E.
Related to Hayes, Roman Pottery in the Royal Ontario Museum, 104, pl. 19.156; Robinson, Athenian Agora V, pl. 18, M 6.

P-54 Piriform unguentarium. Fig. 3

Intact. H. 0.074, D. rim 0.022, D. base 0.006. Clay 5YR 6/2 light olive grey. Semi-coarse clay with fibrous inclusions. Beveled rim with neck tapered to short, angular body. Incised grooves at mid-belly. The shape of this vase is unusual and perhaps has been derived from the piriform unguentarium type; possibly a Palestinian variation of the piriform type.
Late 1st Cent. B.C.E.--1st Cent. C.E.?
Perhaps derived from Pritchard, "Herodian Jericho," AASOR 32-33 (1952-1954) pl. 59.26-27.

P-55 Ribbed unguentarium or balsamarium. Fig. 3

Intact. H. 0.094, D. rim 0.026, D. base 0.027. Clay 7.5YR 6/6 reddish yellow. Semi-fine clay with traces of sand-sized and micaceous inclusions. Tapered and flared upper neck and rim; deep wheel-turned finger grooves on long neck of vessel; short bulbous body with flat base. The shape of this vessel is unusual and has no known ceramic parallels. The rippled contour, however, suggests that it may have originated in blown glass, since it is similar in shape to the corrugated glass balsamarium; perhaps a Palestinian ceramic imitation of the glass balsamarium.
1st Cent. C.E.?
Perhaps derived from A. Kisa, Das Glas im Altertume I (Leipzig 1908) 151, fig. 77.

P-56 Ribbed unguentarium or balsamarium. Fig. 3

Intact. H. 0.096, D. rim 0.027, D. base 0.029. Clay 7.5YR 6/6 reddish yellow. Semi-fine clay with traces of sand-sized and micaceous inclusions. Tapered and beveled upper neck and rim; deep wheel-turned finger grooves over entire vessel; flat base. Similar to P-55.
For date and related shapes, see under P-55.

P-57 Small bulbous unguentarium? Fig. 3

Intact. H. 0.083, D. rim 0.042, D. base 0.028. Clay 10YR 8/3 very pale brown. Fine, well-smoothed clay, flecked with light grey fibrous inclusions. Light brown core. Sharply off-set

rim, wide neck, flared flat base. Plain. The shape of this vase is unusual. It may be derived from the bulbous unguentarium type but has a more flaring base and wide-neck, and lacks a colored wash over the neck; possibly a Palestinian variation of the bulbous type.
Late 1st Cent. B.C.E.--1st Cent. C.E.?
Perhaps derived from Robinson, Athenian Agora V, pl. 2, F 50; pl. 5, G 97.

P-58 Small conical jar or stopper. Fig. 3

Intact. H. 0.059, D. rim 0.038, D. base 0.028. Clay and slip 7.5YR 8/4 pink. Fine fabric with sand-sized inclusions. Everted rim; bulbous carinated body; flat base. Such vessels are used either as stoppers for table amphorae, as at Corinth, or as small jars, perhaps for unguents.
1st-2nd Cent. C.E.
Related to Jones, in Goldman, Tarsus I, 217, fig. 123.93; J.W. Hayes, "Roman Pottery from the South Stoa at Corinth," Hesperia 42 (1973) 465, pl. 80.230.

P-59 Small conical jar or stopper. Fig. 3

Intact. H. 0.047, D. rim 0.033, D. base 0.028. Clay and slip 5YR 8/3 pink. Semi-coarse fabric with sand-sized and small pebble inclusions; slightly worn. Shape like P-58, but squatter.
1st-2nd Cent. C.E.
For related shapes, see under P-58.

P-60 Juglet. Fig. 3

H. (pres.) 0.095, D. rim 0.021, D. base 0.012. Missing rim, neck, and handle. Clay and slip 5YR 7/8 reddish yellow. Semi-coarse fabric with sand-sized and small pebble inclusions. Worn surfaces. Slender cylindrical body with spiral ribbing. Flat base.
3rd-4th Cent. C.E.?
cf. Hayes, Roman Pottery in the Royal Ontario Museum, 120, pl. 35.307.

P-61 Juglet. Fig. 3

H. (pres.) 0.105, D. 0.078, D. base 0.027. Missing rim and handle. Clay 5YR 5/4 reddish brown; slip 10YR 7/4 very pale brown. Semi-fine clay with white micaceous inclusions. Sagging body; tubular neck. Wheel ribbing on belly.
1st Cent. C.E.

cf. Hayes, Roman Pottery in the Royal Ontario Museum, 118, pl. 33.280.

P-62 Juglet. Fig. 3

Intact. H. 0.099, D. 0.061, D. rim 0.038, D. base 0.025. Clay 5YR 7/4; slip 7/5YR 7/4 pink. Coarse fabric with sand-sized and micaceous inclusions. Ovoid body with splayed rim; ribbed handle. Spiral ridging on lower neck and belly.
3rd-4th Cent. C.E.
Related to Hayes, Roman Pottery in the Royal Ontario Museum, 121, pl. 36.312.

P-63 Juglet. Fig. 3

Intact. H. 0.085, D. 0.054, D. rim 0.036, D. base 0.021. Clay 2.5YR 6/8 light red; slip 10YR 4/6 dark yellowish brown; Similar to P-62 but with spiral ridging on entire neck and belly.
For date and related shapes, see under P-62.

P-64 Juglet. Fig. 3

Intact. H. 0.09, D. 0.06, D. rim 0.032, D. base 0.025. Clay 7.5YR 8/4 pink; slip 7.5YR 5/8 strong brown. Similar to P-62, but with a more sagging body.
For date and related shapes, see under P-62.

P-65 Juglet. Fig. 3

Intact. H. 0.095, D. 0.064, D. rim 0.038, D. base 0.029. Clay 5YR 7/4 pink; slip 7.5YR 5/8 strong brown. Similar to P-62, but with spiral ridging on belly only.
For date and related shapes, see under P-62.

P-66 Juglet. Fig. 3

Restored. H. 0.084, D. 0.059, D. rim 0.041, D. base 0.027. Clay 10YR 7/6 yellow; slip 10YR 6/1 grey. Slightly blackened by fire. Similar to P-62, but smaller and with broad spiral ridging on lower belly only.
For date and related shapes, see under P-62.

P-67 Juglet. Fig. 3

Intact. H. 0.059, D. rim 0.046, D. base 0.027. Clay 7.5YR 8/4 pink; slip 10YR 5/8 yellowish brown. Semi-coarse fabric with sand-sized inclusions. Wide neck; short carinated body.

3rd Cent. C.E.
Related to U. Hölscher, <u>The Excavations of Medinet Habu</u> V, <u>Post Ramesside Remains</u> (Chicago 1954), pl. 48.N'4.

P-68 Ribbed juglet. Fig. 3

Intact. H. 0.064, D. rim 0.035, D. base 0.024. Clay 2.5YR 6/6 light reddish brown. Semi-fine clay; wet-smoothed surface with sand and micaceous inclusions. Light brown core. Beveled rim with tapered neck and deep wheel-turned finger grooves on body. Flat base; small handle attached to lower neck and upper belly. The shape of this juglet is unusual and may have been derived from small ribbed jars; perhaps a Palestinian variation of the late Roman ribbed jug shape.
3rd-4th Cent. C.E.?
Perhaps derived from Kenyon, <u>Jericho</u> II, 534, fig. 274.8; W.M.F. Petrie, <u>Ehnasya</u> (London 1905) pl. 33.115.

P-69 Small flask. Fig. 3

Restored. H. 0.088, D. rim 0.017, D. base 0.019. Missing one handle. Clay and slip 2.5YR 6/8 light red. Coarse fabric with sand-sized and small pebble inclusions; worn surfaces. Short neck, round body, flat base.
3rd Cent. C.E.
Related to U. Hölscher, <u>Medinet Habu</u> V, pl.; 48.L'2.

P-70 Small flask. Fig. 3

Restored. H. 0.079, D. rim 0.020, D. base 0.017. Missing one handle and portion of rim. Clay and slip 7.5YR 7/6 reddish yellow. Coarse fabric with sand-sized and pebble inclusions. Very short neck, round body, small flat base.
3rd Cent. C.E.
Related to P-69, but with neck handles attached to rim.

<u>Byzantine</u>

P-71 Juglet. Fig. 3

Intact. H. 0.07, D. 0.048, D. rim 0.016, D. base 0.021. Clay 5YR 7/8 to 7.5YR 7/6 reddish yellow. Semi-coarse clay with sand-sized inclusions; worn surfaces. String cut flat base; handle from rim to shoulder; broad body with beveled rim. Decorated on shoulder with diagonal grooves in groups of two and three.

6th Cent. C.E.
cf. Hayes, Roman Pottery in the Royal Ontario Museum, 123, pl. 38.355; P. Delougaz and R.C. Haines, A Byzantine Church at Khirbet al-Karak (Chicago 1960) pls. 34.1, 56.8; H. Kantor, Soundings at Tell Fakhariyah (Chicago 1958) 36, pl. 33.75; Crowfoot et al., Samaria-Sebaste III, 362-3, fig. 84a.3.

II. LAMPS

Iron Age

L-1 Lamp. Fig. 4

Restored. H. 0.055, W. 0.135. Clay 5YR 5/8 yellowish red. Portion of body and lip broken near spout. Semi-coarse clay with fine straw inclusions and small mineral grit. Some incrustation on surface; spout blackened from burning. No traces of slip preserved. Wide lip, deep bowl, rounded base.
Beer-Sheba, Locus 881, registration no. 8058/1.
Iron IIA-B.
cf. Yadin et al., Hazor III-IV, pl. 208.47 (Hazor IX).

L-2 Lamp. Fig. 4

Intact. H. 0.039, W. 0.134. Clay 5YR 5/6 yellowish red. Semi-coarse clay with some straw inclusions and large mineral grit. Surfaces pock marked and weathered. Spout blackened from burning. Everted rim, shallow bowl, flat base.
Iron IIC.
cf. Yadin et al., Hazor II, pl. 88.13 (Hazor VA).

L-3 Lamp. Fig. 4

Intact. H. 0.053, W. 0.13, D. base 0.059. Clay 5YR 7/6 reddish yellow. Coarse clay with straw inclusions and large mineral grit. Surfaces heavily pockmarked and quite worn. Spout blackened from burning. Deep bowl, high disc base.
Iron IIC.
cf. Albright, "Beit Mirsim I," AASOR 12 (1930-31) pl. 70.4.

L-4 Lamp. Fig. 4

Intact. H. 0.04, W. 0.131. Clay 5YR 5/8 yellowish red. Semi-coarse to medium fabric with some straw inclusions and very fine mineral grit. Good smooth surfaces. No traces of burning

around spout, so lamp probably never used. Everted rim, flat base (similar to L-2).
Iron IIC.
cf. Lamon and Shipton, Megiddo I, pl. 37.13 (Megiddo IV-III).

L-5 Lamp. Fig. 4

Restored. H. 0.063, W. 0.13, D. base 0.059. Clay and slip 2.5YR 5/8 red. Missing portion of rim near spout and part of back. Semi-coarse clay with some straw inclusions and coarse mineral grit. Some incrustation on surface. Traces of red slip preserved. Spout blackened from burning. Deep bowl, high disc base.
7th Cent. B.C.E.
cf. Tufnell and Harding, Lachish III, pl. 83.151 (Lachish II).

Roman

L-6 Spout frag. of lamp. Fig. 4

H. (pres.) 0.031, W. (pres.) 0.04. Clay and slip 7.5YR 5/4 brown. Mould-made. Semi-coarse to medium fine fabric with micaceous inclusions. Good surfaces. Traces of brown slip preserved. Shape similar to that of bow-spouted ("Herodian") lamps.
Mid-1st Cent. C.E.
cf. Pritchard, "Herodian Jericho," AASOR 32-33 (1952-54) pl. 59.32-33.

Byzantine

L-7 Lamp. Fig. 4

Restored. H. 0.039, H. with handle 0.052, W. 0.096. Clay and slip 10YR 5/2 grayish brown. Mould-made. Semi-coarse to medium fine clay with small micaceous inclusions. Traces of brown slip preserved. Ovoid nozzle with raised lines from central opening to nozzle. Decoration of 2 rosettes on top and rosettes within circles around shoulder. Underside of base decorated with row of concentric circles and 3 lines radiating from center.
8th-9th Cent. C.E.
cf. Crowfoot et al., Samaria-Sebaste III, 375-76, fig. 89.9.

L-8 Lamp. Fig. 4

Intact. H. 0.101, D. base 0.062, D. rim 0.047, L. spout 0.045. Clay 5YR 7/3 pink; core 5YR 7/4 pink. Chipped at rim. Coarse clay with sand-sized and small pebble inclusions. Green glaze preserved on body near handle. Sagging body with short neck. The spout, open on top, is located near the base of the vessel and is burnt at its tip.
Byzantine.
Related to F.O. Waage, in _Antioch on-the-Orantes_ III (Princeton 1941) Type 61, no. 190, figs. 83, 87; C.A. Kennedy, "The Development of the Lamp in Palestine," _Berytus_ 14 (1963) 81, 105 and pl. 25, no. 630. For similar glaze, cf. C.H. Morgan II, _Corinth_ XI, _The Byzantine Pottery_ (Harvard 1942) no. 300.

III.FIGURINES

Bronze Age

F-1 Basalt base with foot. Fig. 5

Base about ½ preserved; foot broken above ankle. H. (pres.) 0.073, W. (pres.) 0.084. Color 5YR 4/1 dark grey. Smooth surfaces with a few fine scratches. Left foot preserved; heel, ankle, and toes well defined and precisely carved. Probably part of larger votive offering of the Pharaonic type.
LB II.
cf. Yadin _et al._, _Hazor_ III-IV, pls. 323.6, 324.4-6.

Iron Age

F-2 Frag. of terracotta incense burner. Fig. 5

Female figurine attached to pillar standing on lion. Lion missing legs; broken at point where pillar joins lion. Figurine and pillar: H. 0.151, W. 0.063. Lion: H. (pres.) 0.058, W. 0.081. Clay and slip 5YR 6/6 reddish yellow. Semi-coarse fabric with some straw inclusions and mineral grit. Lion extremely worn with eroded surfaces. Traces of reddish-yellow slip preserved. Hair of figurine has 2 spiral ringlets in the Hathor style; face has heavy rounded chin, prominent ears, protruding almond-shaped eyes. Necklace around neck; hands hold breasts; triple girdle at waist, triple anklets.

Tail of lion curves around back. Possibly from a house-shaped incense burner.
Iron I-II.
cf. Amrian, 305, photo 347 (face) (Megiddo): Crowfoot *et al.*, *Samaria-Sebaste* III, 79, no. 1 (C 1270), pl. 11.6 (body); Yadin *et al.*, *Hazor* III-IV, pls. 314.2-3; 356.9.

F-3 Frag. of terracotta incense burner. Fig. 5

Female figurine attached to pillar standing on lion. Figurine broken at feet; lion complete with base. Figurine and pillar: H. (pres.) 0.119, W. (pres.) 0.056. Lion: H. 0.098, W. 0.073, W. with base 0.099. Clay and slip 5YR 5/6 yellowish red. Semi-coarse fabric with fine straw inclusions and coarse mineral grit. Worn and flaky surfaces. Traces of yellowish slip preserved.
Description similar to F-2.
Date and parallels as F-2.

Hellenistic

F-4 Bronze bell. Fig. 5

Intact, but missing clapper. H. 0.037, W. 0.026. Heavily corroded. Conical shaped with loop handle for suspension.
Late Hellenistic-Roman.
cf. Crowfoot *et al.*, *Samaria-Sebaste* III, 429, fig. 100, no. 22 (bracelet with attached bell from Tomb E 220): related to Robinson, *Athenian Agora* V, pl. 53, J 17.

F-5 Bronze head. Fig. 5

Broken at neck. H. (pres.) 0.031, W. 0.03. Corroded, but facial features easily distinguishable. Chin slightly pointed and tilted, eyes not well defined, nose prominent, cheeks full and rounded, hair parted almost at center of head.
Late Hellenistic.
cf. Crowfoot *et al.*, *Samaria-Sebaste* III, 83, no. 5 (Qe 1088), pl. 13.5.

University of Minnesota
1 February 1984

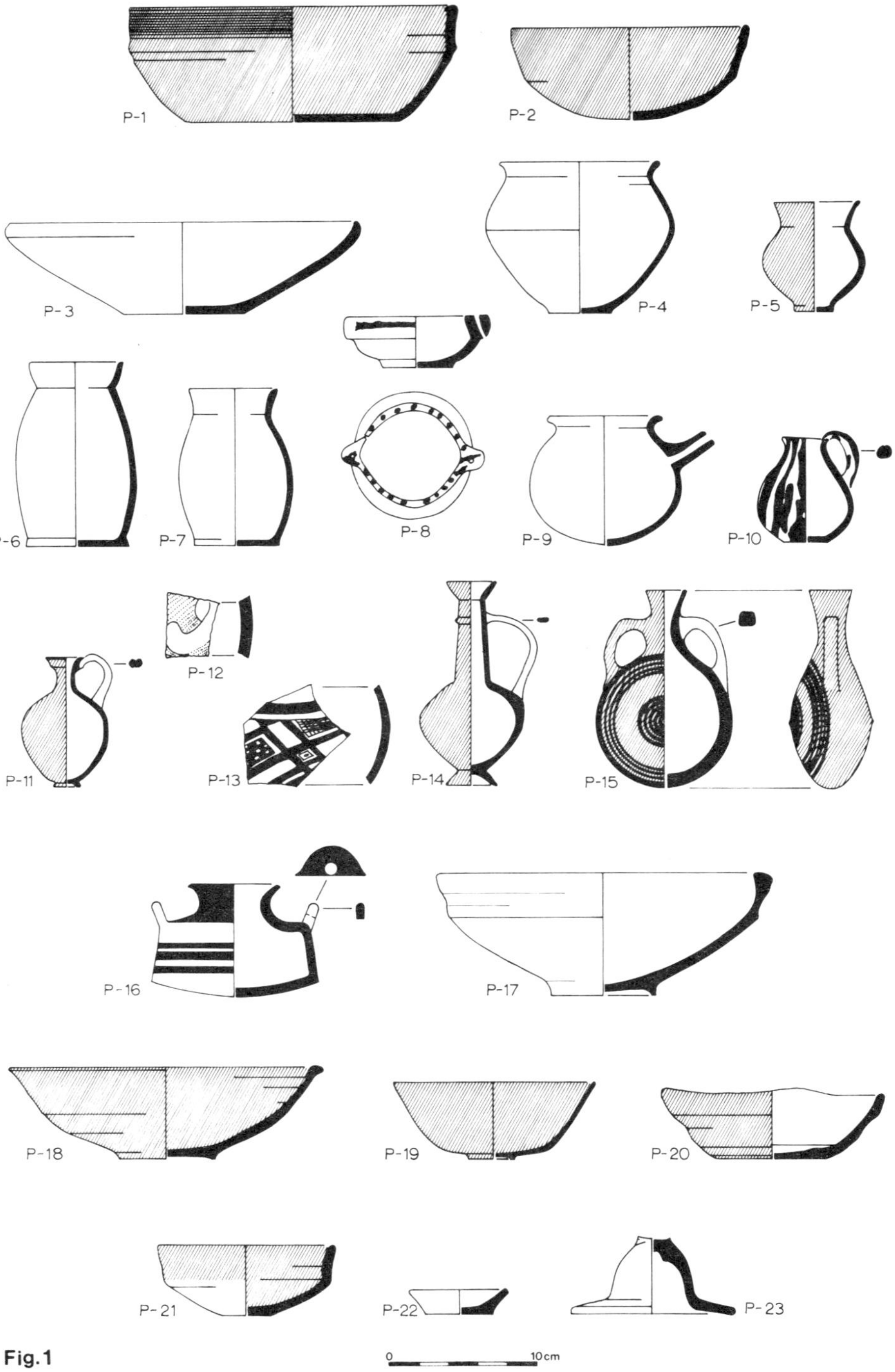
P-1
P-2
P-3
P-4
P-5
P-6
P-7
P-8
P-9
P-10
P-11
P-12
P-13
P-14
P-15
P-16
P-17
P-18
P-19
P-20
P-21
P-22
P-23
0
10cm

Fig. 1

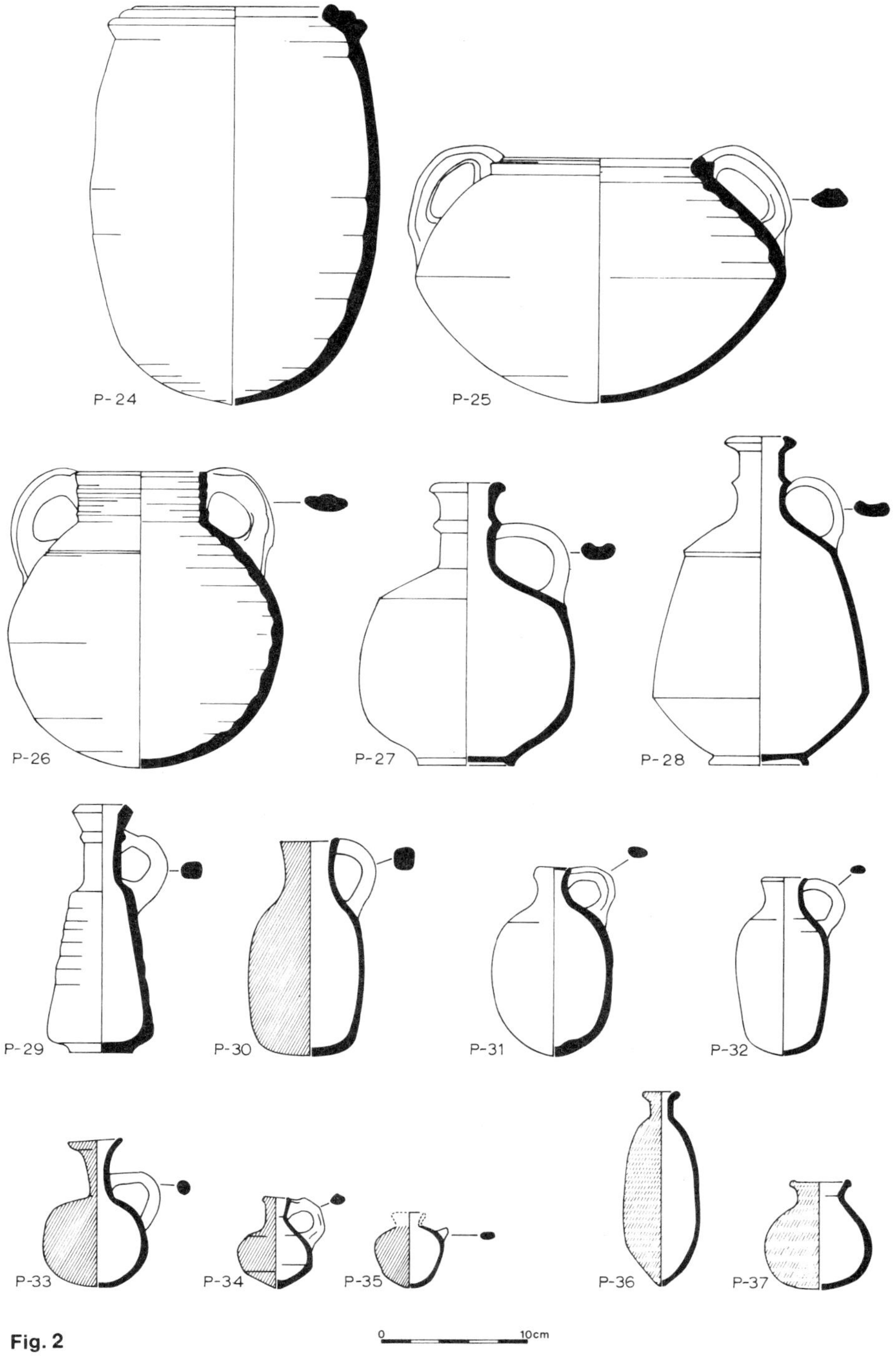

Fig. 2

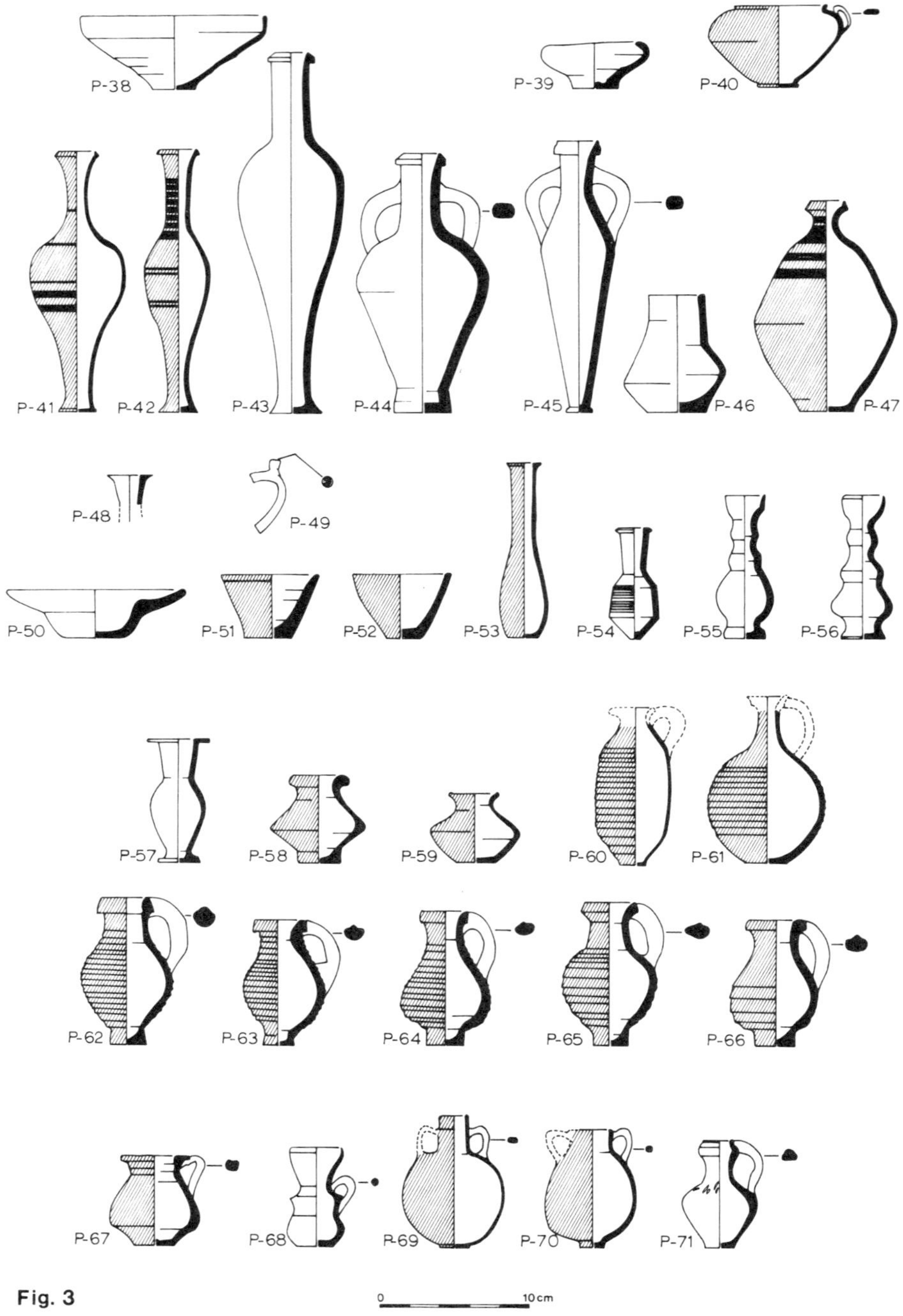
P-38
P-39
P-40
P-41
P-42
P-43
P-44
P-45
P-46
P-47
P-48
P-49
P-50
P-51
P-52
P-53
P-54
P-55
P-56
P-57
P-58
P-59
P-60
P-61
P-62
P-63
P-64
P-65
P-66
P-67
P-68
P-69
P-70
P-71
0
10cm

Fig. 3

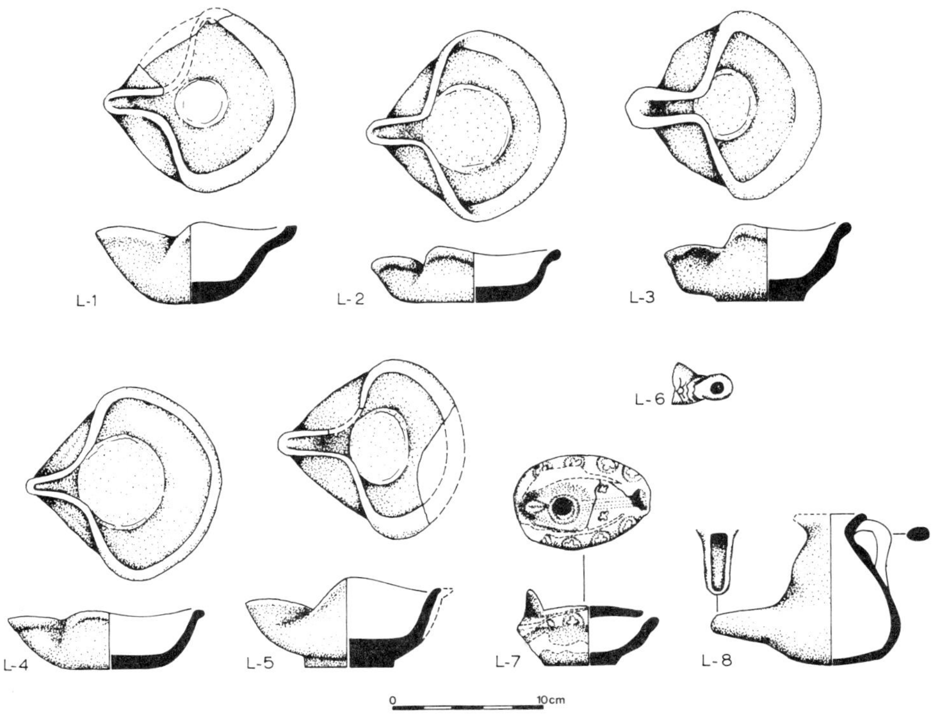

Fig. 4

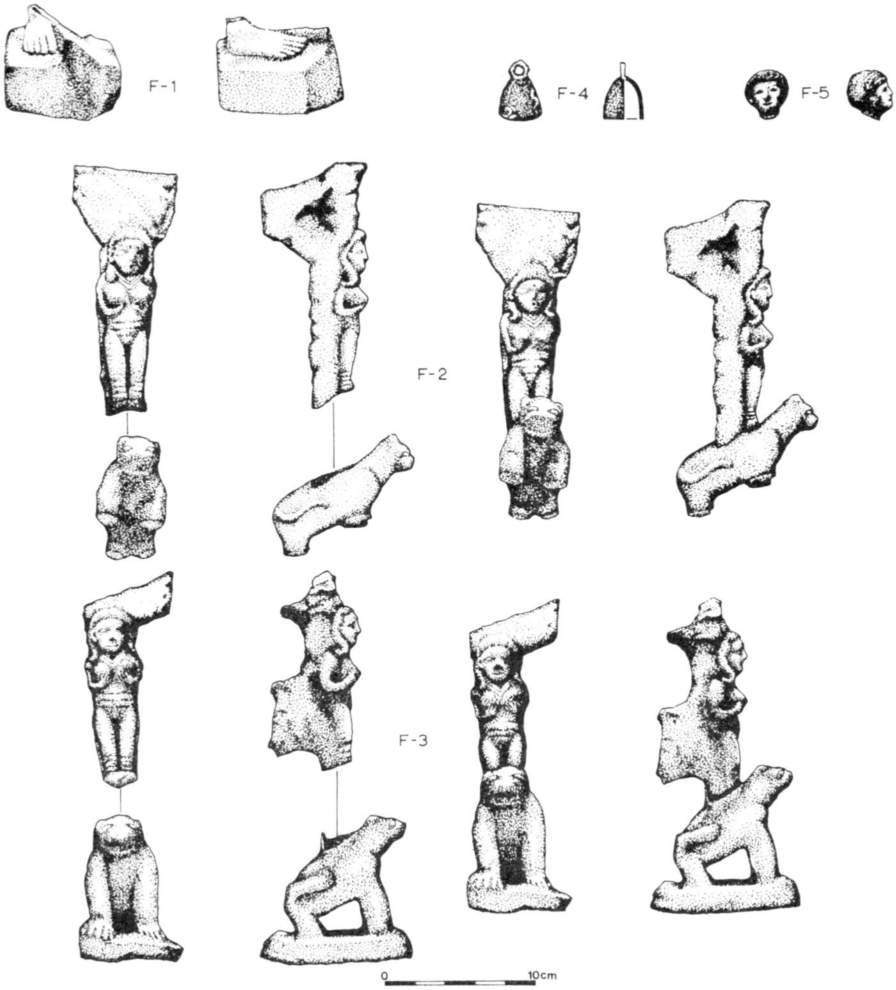

Fig. 5